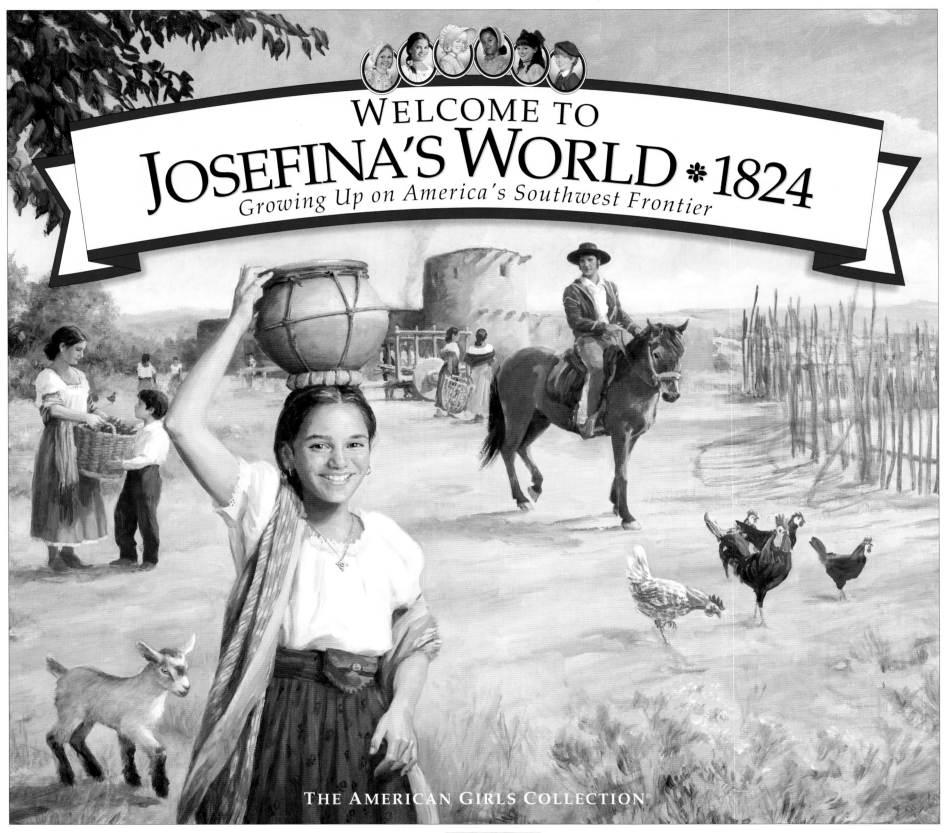

WELCOME TO
JOSEFINA'S WORLD ✻ 1824
Growing Up on America's Southwest Frontier

THE AMERICAN GIRLS COLLECTION®

Published by Pleasant Company Publications
© Copyright 1999 by Pleasant Company
All rights reserved. No part of this book may be used or reproduced
in any manner whatsoever without written permission except in the
case of brief quotations embodied in critical articles and reviews.
For information, address: Book Editor,
Pleasant Company Publications,
8400 Fairway Place, P.O. Box 620998,
Middleton, WI 53562.

Printed in Singapore
99 00 01 02 03 04 05 TWP 10 9 8 7 6 5 4 3 2 1
The American Girls Collection®, the American Girl logo, Josefina®,
and Josefina Montoya® are trademarks of Pleasant Company.

Written by Yvette La Pierre
Edited by Jodi Evert and Peg Ross
Historical and Editorial Consulting by American Historical Publications
Designed and Art Directed by Kristyn Kalnes, Mengwan Lin, and Jane S. Varda
Produced by Mary Cudnohfsky, Cheryll Mellenthin, and Paula Moon
Cover Illustration by Jean-Paul Tibbles
Interior Illustrations by Laszlo Kubinyi, Susan McAliley, Susan Moore, and Jean-Paul Tibbles
Researched by Rebecca Bernstein, Kathy Borkowski, Mary Davison, and Sally Jacobs
Photography by Jamie Young
Prop Research and Styling by Jean doPico

Library of Congress Cataloging-in-Publication Data

Welcome to Josefina's World, 1824 — growing up on America's Southwest frontier /
p. cm. — (The American girls collection)
Summary: Describes the daily life and activities of Mexican Americans in
New Mexico during the early 1800s including information about their homes,
community, and links to Spain and Mexico.
ISBN 1-56247-769-2
1. Mexican Americans—New Mexico—Social life and customs—19th century Juvenile literature.
2. Mexican Americans—New Mexico—Social conditions—19th century Juvenile literature.
3. New Mexico—History—To 1848 Juvenile literature. 4. New Mexico—Social life and customs—
19th century Juvenile literature. 5. Girls—New Mexico—Social life and customs—19th century
Juvenile literature. 6. Girls—New Mexico—Social life and customs—19th century Juvenile literature.
[1. Mexican Americans—New Mexico. 2. New Mexico—History—To 1848. 3. New Mexico—
Social life and customs—19th century.] I. Title: Welcome to Josefina's world II. Series.
F800 .W45 1999 978.9'03—dc21 99-26634 CIP

Table of Contents

Welcome to Josefina's World

What Josefina wanted most was for her sisters to be at peace with one another. She wanted the household to be running smoothly, and Papá to be happy and laughing again. She longed for life to be the way it was when Mamá was alive.

—Meet Josefina

❋

After Mamá died, Josefina cherished a carved wooden box that had belonged to Mamá. Josefina called it her "memory box" because inside she kept things that reminded her of Mamá. Whenever Josefina opened it, the scent of Mamá's lavender soap and the sight of the primroses Mamá had loved gave Josefina comfort.

Josefina and her sisters struggled to keep things as they were when Mamá was alive. The sisters worked hard at their chores, remembered the prayers and songs Mamá had taught them, and followed the traditions she had loved. Josefina took comfort in the familiar rhythm of life on Papá's *rancho* (RAHN-cho), or farm, in northern New Mexico.

Then her grandfather's trading caravan from Mexico City arrived with a surprise that would soon change their lives—their mother's sister, Tía Dolores.  Tía Dolores brought new ideas and fresh ways of doing things to the rancho. She even taught the sisters how to read and write, something Mamá had never learned. Josefina was excited about these changes, but she worried that they might make her forget Mamá.

At the same time, another change was spreading through Josefina's world. By 1824, American traders had begun traveling to New Mexico. Josefina and her sisters couldn't wait to see the fine and fancy things the traders would bring. But American customs and manners seemed strange, and many New Mexicans were not sure Americans could be trusted. Most New Mexicans were both curious and cautious. They wondered what changes, both for better and for worse, these newcomers would bring.

Cities Made of Gold

Three hundred years before Josefina's story begins, Spanish soldiers claimed Mexico as a colony of Spain. New Mexico was uncharted territory in the northern part of Mexico. Spanish explorers heard a rumor that seven golden cities lay hidden in those northern lands. In 1540, the explorers set out to find them.

Instead of cities made of gold, the explorers found Pueblo Indian villages made of earth. Native Americans had been living on this land for thousands of years.

Indians painted pictures of the Spaniards on rocks.

Spanish explorers wore armor to protect themselves against possible attacks.

MORE PRECIOUS THAN GOLD
The explorers returned with news of something more precious than gold—land to settle. Soon settlers from Spain and Mexico began trickling into New Mexico with the dream of owning their own land.

The Spanish introduced horses to New Mexico. At first, some Indians thought these huge, armored animals were man-eating beasts.

FORCED LABOR

The Spanish forced Indians to do much of their labor in building churches. Indians who resisted were beaten, and some had their hands or feet cut off.

SETTLERS

In 1598, Spanish families arrived in New Mexico. They had journeyed 1,500 miles, mostly on foot. Catholic priests came, too. Their mission was to serve the settlers and bring the Catholic faith to the Indians.

REVOLT

After 70 years of attack and harsh treatment by the Spanish, the peaceful Pueblo Indians finally rebelled in 1680. They attacked and killed settlers and priests and burned homes, farms, and churches, driving the Spaniards from their land.

The settlers began to build New Mexico's capital city of Santa Fe in about 1608. Santa Fe is the oldest capital city in America.

FINDING PEACE

The Spanish recaptured New Mexico in 1692. This time, the Spanish treated the Pueblo Indians more fairly. Gradually, the two peoples learned to live as neighbors.

These Pueblo Indians have invited their neighbors to watch a Corn Dance.

A Rich Mix

For hundreds of years, New Mexico was a Spanish and Indian world. Spanish rulers did not allow foreigners, including Americans, to trade there. Spain wanted to keep tight control over this faraway part of its empire. New Mexico's only link to the outside world was the *Camino Real* (kah-MEE-no rey-AHL), the 1,600-mile wagon trail from Mexico City to Santa Fe.

Then, in 1821, when Josefina was six years old, Mexico won its freedom from Spain. The Mexican government allowed New Mexicans to trade with foreigners. Almost immediately, American traders began blazing the Santa Fe Trail, which led from Missouri to New Mexico. When they reached New Mexico, they found a rich mix of Spanish, Mexican, and Indian cultures. American goods and ideas soon became part of that mix.

① **MEXICO CITY**
Mexico City, the sophisticated capital of Mexico, was a center of international trade. Goods from all over the world traveled up the Camino Real to New Mexico.

② **PUEBLO INDIANS**
Pueblo Indians have lived in New Mexico for thousands of years. They lived in apartment-style earth homes and made their living by farming. The Pueblo Indians and the Spanish often fought together against enemies.

4

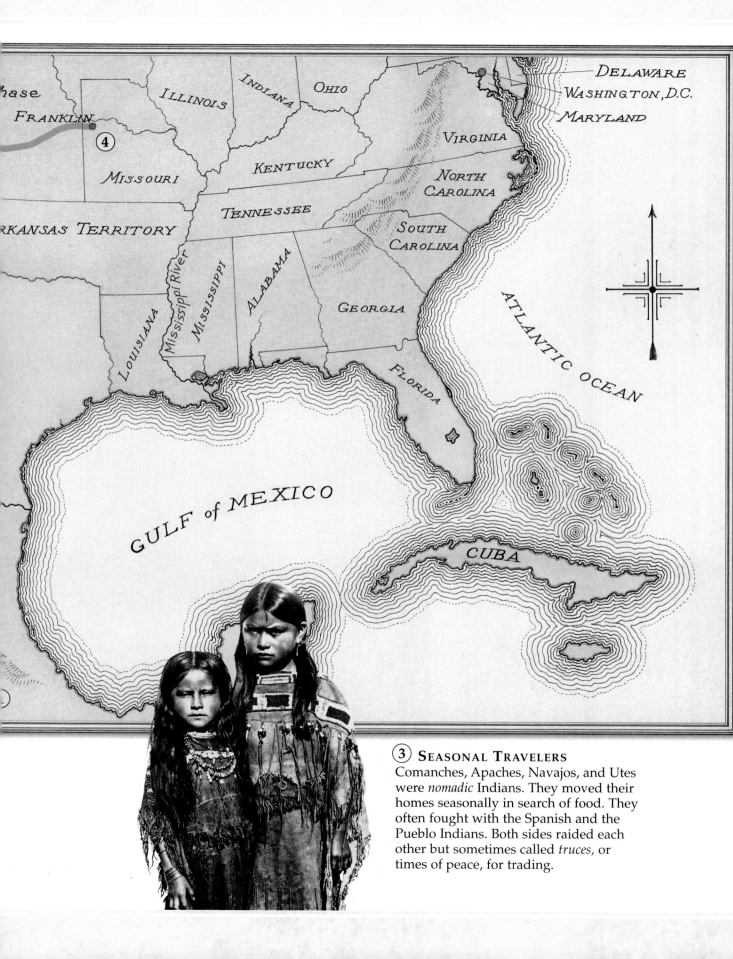

DELAWARE
WASHINGTON, D.C.
MARYLAND

ILLINOIS INDIANA OHIO

hase
FRANKLIN
④

MISSOURI

KENTUCKY

VIRGINIA

NORTH
CAROLINA

RKANSAS TERRITORY

TENNESSEE

SOUTH
CAROLINA

LOUISIANA

Mississippi River

MISSISSIPPI

ALABAMA

GEORGIA

FLORIDA

ATLANTIC OCEAN

GULF of MEXICO

CUBA

⑤ SANTA FE
When American traders arrived in Santa Fe's dusty marketplace, they found Spanish settlers, Pueblo Indians, French fur trappers, Comanches, Apaches, Navajos, and Utes trading goods from all around the world.

④ BLAZING THE TRAIL
Franklin, Missouri, was one of the *trailheads,* or starting points, of the Santa Fe Trail. Each spring, American traders loaded their wagons and began the dangerous two-month journey to Santa Fe.

③ SEASONAL TRAVELERS
Comanches, Apaches, Navajos, and Utes were *nomadic* Indians. They moved their homes seasonally in search of food. They often fought with the Spanish and the Pueblo Indians. Both sides raided each other but sometimes called *truces,* or times of peace, for trading.

5

Land of Enchantment

Like the Indians before them, Spanish settlers built homes in the mountains and valleys of the Rio Grande, the biggest river in New Mexico. From Papá's rancho, Josefina could see dry, rugged land stretching for miles. On the eastern horizon, rolling foothills covered with dark green pines met high mountains that pierced the clear blue sky.

In the winter, the mountains were capped with snow. When the snow melted in the spring, it flowed down into cold rivers and streams, bringing precious water to the parched lands below. Both Indians and settlers relied on these rivers and streams for all their water needs. Josefina knew that the old saying *"El agua es la vida"* was true. Water was life to this land. Nothing could survive without it.

Houses of Earth

New Mexican settlers created homes out of the earth and water of their new land. Just as they had done in Mexico and Spain, they mixed mud and straw to make *adobe* (ah-DOH-beh), which they molded into bricks and dried in the sun. They stacked the bricks to form walls and used mud to hold the bricks together. The thick walls kept families warm during the chilly winters and cool during the hot summers. New Mexican settlers who lived outside the safety of a town or village built their homes like fortresses. In case of attack by unfriendly Indians, people and animals were gathered inside and the front gate locked tight.

1 *The early Spanish settlers were amazed to find that Pueblo Indians built their homes out of adobe, too.*

2 *Settlers made fences by lashing sticks together with wet rawhide. The rawhide tightened as it dried, holding the sticks firmly in place.*

3 *A small herd of goats near the house provided milk to drink and to make into cheese.*

COURTYARD
In Josefina's time, houses were often built around an inner courtyard. For added protection, the doors of each room opened onto the courtyard, rather than to the outside.

WINDOWS
The small, high windows let in light and air, but not enemy invaders. This window has bars on it. The other windows are made from a see-through mineral called *mica*.

FRONT GATE
The heavy front gate could open wide enough to let in wagons pulled by oxen. Most times, people used the small door within the gate to enter the courtyard.

ROOF
The roof was made by laying slender logs across the width of the house. Brush was piled on top of the logs, then a layer of adobe, and finally eight or more inches of dirt.

④ *Waterspouts helped drain water from the flat roof.*

WATCHTOWER
Settlers could see friends or enemies coming for many miles from the narrow window in the watchtower.

CRACKS
Each spring, the women and children put a new coat of adobe plaster on the walls to repair cracks. Children liked to spread the mud with their bare hands.

TRACKS
Wagon tracks show that this home had many visitors. Ranchos along the Camino Real often hosted caravans of traveling traders.

From Dawn to Dusk

Each morning, settlers rose early to the sound of the village's church bell calling them to another day of work. In the 1820s most New Mexicans lived in small villages or on nearby ranchos. Rancho families lived in homes like this one, along with relatives, servants, and farmworkers. Settlers worked hard from dawn to dusk to get everything they needed from the land. Girls like Josefina helped run the house, while the men and boys worked in the fields. Each day—and the changing seasons—brought chores for everyone in the family.

COURTYARD

Most of the household activity took place in the courtyard, or *placita* (plah-SEE-tah). Girls and women husked corn, tended children, and strung fresh chiles and other vegetables to dry in the sun.

COCINA

The kitchen, or *cocina* (ko-SEE-nah), was busy from before dawn until after dusk. Women spent hours preparing enough food to feed everyone on the rancho. They talked, sang, and told stories as they worked.

Watchtower

1 *Settlers didn't need many chairs because they built **bancos** (BAHN-kohs), or low benches, into the walls of their homes.*

2 *Dried vegetables, fruits, grains, and meats were kept in a cool storage room for use throughout the winter.*

*Bread was baked in outdoor ovens called **hornos** (OR-nohs).*

⑤ *Wooden beds were rare in New Mexico. This one was probably reserved for guests or an elderly relative.*

Red dye was made from insects that lived on cactus plants.

WEAVING ROOM
The family used wool from the rancho's sheep to weave colorful blankets and rugs for the household, plus extras to trade.

*Checked **jerga** (HEHR-gah) cloths were woven from undyed sheep's wool.*

④ *Herbs and other plants were used for cooking, dyes, and medicine.*

ROLLAWAY BEDS
The first task of each day was to roll up the beds, which were soft sheepskins covered with wool blankets. The sleeping rooms could then be used for other activities during the day.

Corner fireplaces *were used for heating, cooking, and light.*

FAMILY ALTAR
The village church bells rang each morning, noon, and evening to call the families to their altars for prayer.

*Sometimes sick goats and sheep slept inside on the **shepherd's bed**, a warm shelf above the kitchen fireplace.*

③ *The hanging light is called an **araña** (ah-RAH-nya), the Spanish word for spider. It dangled from the ceiling just like a spider!*

Faith

New Mexicans relied on their strong faith in God to help them survive the hardships of their lives. Every church and almost every room in the house had *santos* (SAHN-tohs), or images of saints.

The Catholic saints were very important to New Mexicans. Families asked saints for help with daily struggles, large and small. Saint Anthony of Padua, for example, helped find lost animals, Saint Apollonia protected against toothaches, and Saint Roch saved people from diseases.

A PLACE OF HEALING
This church in Chimayó, New Mexico, was built in 1813 on the spot where a miracle was believed to have happened. It is considered a place of great healing. Thousands of people still make holy journeys to Chimayó today.

HIDE PAINTING
Early Spanish settlers and priests brought religious images painted on easy-to-carry buffalo or deer hides. The images were often used to teach local Indians about the Catholic faith.

BULTO
Statues of saints are called *bultos* (BOOL-tohs). This bulto of the Virgin Mary has a crescent moon on the skirt to symbolize purity.

Settlers pinned small silver medals on a santo to give thanks or make requests such as sending rain, helping crops, or healing an animal.

RETABLO
Images of saints painted on flat wood panels are called *retablos* (reh-TAH-blohs). This small retablo may have been put in its pouch and taken along on a journey.

ALTAR SCREEN
Tall, decorative screens often graced church altars. This screen features elegant figures painted by José Rafael Aragón, a famous religious artist in Josefina's time.

The Art of Faith

When Josefina was a girl, many *santeros* (sahn-TEH-rohs), or religious artists, traveled from village to village seeking work. The villagers were always happy to see a santero arrive. Along with the tools and supplies packed on his burro, the santero brought news from other villages. He went from door to door, and the villagers ordered a painting or statue of their favorite saint.

The santero cut down pine trees to make flat panels or dug up the roots of cottonwood trees to carve into statues. After carving a statue or smoothing the surface of a wood panel, he painted the surface with a white coating called *gesso* (JEH-soh). Then he applied paints made from minerals and plants. Even his paintbrushes were handmade—yucca fronds or willow shoots, chicken feathers bound together, or animal hair tied into neat bunches.

Villagers paid the santero with food, tools, clothing, or a small amount of money. Sometimes a village family gave him room and board as payment for his work. Then he packed up his burro and headed to the next village.

Woodworking tools

Carved and ready for painting

Finished statue

Beauty in a Harsh Land

Spanish and Indian craftsmen turned to the land around them to find the raw materials to make beautiful household goods. They used plants and earth to fashion baskets and pots. Carpenters built furniture from yellow pine and used wooden pegs to hold the furniture together. Weavers used plants and minerals to make dyes for wool. Their blankets were as beautiful as the land they came from!

GOLDEN PATTERNS
New Mexican artisans didn't have mother-of-pearl to create designs set in wood, a style popular in Europe. Instead they pasted bits of straw or cornhusk to create golden patterns.

BEAUTY INSIDE AND OUT
Cabinets were richly decorated with hand carving and colorful paints, even on the inside. They often had secret compartments to hide the family's best silver.

WRITING DESKS
Writing desks looked like small, plain chests from the outside. They opened to reveal beautiful painting and many tiny drawers.

WOVEN BLANKETS
To make blankets, girls and women first *carded*, or untangled, raw wool with brushes ①. After dyeing the wool ② and spinning it into yarn ③, it was ready for the loom ④.

Blankets were hung on the wall to brighten a room and add an extra layer of protection from the cold.

BASKETS
New Mexicans traded for Pueblo baskets. This one is made of willow, a tree that grows along streams and has flexible branches.

COLCHA
New Mexican women and girls did *colcha* (KOHL-chah) embroidery in the evening by firelight. Stitches were often different lengths because they could hardly see their sewing.

POTTERY
This Pueblo jar is narrow at the top to make it easier to carry water without spilling. It has a slight hollow in the bottom so it can balance easily on the head.

Loving Jewel

When a baby was born, he or she was immediately welcomed into the community and the church. Shortly after the birth, a girl or boy was sent to every home in the village to announce the baby's arrival. A few days later, the baby was *baptized,* or made a member of the Catholic Church. After this important ceremony, everyone gathered for feasting and dancing to celebrate the new arrival.

Sleep my beautiful baby,
Sleep my grain of gold...
—A New Mexican Lullaby

BRINGING BABIES INTO THE WORLD
Babies were delivered by a *partera* (pahr-TEH-rah), a woman skilled at helping mothers and babies during childbirth. The partera was a very respected person in the village.

Older sisters helped take care of the babies in a family.

Babies wore a string of coral beads for good luck.

A SOFT SWING
Hanging cradles swung gently from ceiling beams. The sheepskin lining kept babies cozy.

THE HOLY FAMILY
This religious carving shows the Holy Family— Joseph, Mary, and baby Jesus. It reminded New Mexicans of the importance of family.

Baptism Clothes

The godparents provided all the clothing for the baby's baptism—the cap, gown, shoes, blanket, and even the diapers!

Baptism gown

Special Gifts

Wealthy godparents might have given an exquisite gown or cap from Spain or delicately embroidered slippers as baptism gifts.

Godparents

Godparents helped raise and care for their godchildren all their lives. They even promised to take over as parents if the child was orphaned.

Only the godparents attended the baptism. The rest of the family stayed home and prepared a feast. After the baptism, children ran to meet the godparents, shouting, *"La pastilla! La pastilla!"* The godparents handed out *pastillas* (pahs-TEE-yahs), or little cookies, to celebrate the baby's birth. Then they led the villagers to the parents' house, where they announced, "Here is this loving jewel just come from the church!" Then everyone came inside for food, music, and dancing.

Childhood

From the book Happy Birthday, Josefina!

Children began working when they were very young. Girls fetched water, tended animals, and helped with laundry, weaving, sewing, gardening, and cooking. Boys chopped wood and helped with the planting and harvesting. Few children attended school in Josefina's time, but they sometimes learned to read and write at home. Despite a full day of work and lessons, children still found time for fun.

This girl is sewing in the courtyard of her house.

Josefina thought the chore of replastering the church walls was great fun. She scooped up a handful of mud plaster and flung it at the wall, where it stuck—splat!— in a glob.

IMAGINATION
Children used their imagination to make toys for themselves. They turned scraps of material into dolls, and pieces of bark into toy boats.

GAMES
In warm weather, New Mexican boys played ball games such as *shinny*, a Pueblo Indian game similar to field hockey. On cold winter nights, children often played clapping games before the fire.

READY TO RUN
Fathers sometimes carved toys for their children, like this handmade horse with movable legs.

PUPPETS

Traveling puppet troupes were a rare treat. They put on skits with stringed puppets, or *marionettes.* This is the knight and his horse from the Spanish novel *Don Quixote.*

SAINT'S DAY

Instead of birthdays, children celebrated the feast day of the saint they were named after. Children received small gifts on this special day. They also had the honor of giving gifts like coins or chocolate.

Josefina was named after Saint Joseph, whose feast day is March 19.

CHRISTMAS TREATS

On January 6, families celebrated the Feast of the Three Kings, which honors the Bible story of the kings riding their camels to see baby Jesus. The night before the feast, children left straw in their shoes to feed the camels. By morning, the straw had been replaced with sweets!

FIRST COMMUNION

A girl celebrated her First Communion when she was 12 or 13. To prepare, she learned the prayers and teachings of the Catholic faith. The ceremony marked the first time she could join the adults and receive Holy Communion, or blessed bread and wine, during church services.

Courtship and Marriage

A young girl practices her dance steps.

I n Josefina's time, girls and young women were rarely allowed to go out by themselves. Dances were one of the few places where young people could meet and court. A visitor to Mexico commented that "young people have so few opportunities of being together that Mexican marriages must be made in heaven, for I see no opportunity of bringing them about upon earth!"

PROPOSAL
Marriages were arranged between families. A young man's father and uncles or his godfather called on the girl's father and gave him a formal letter proposing the marriage.

INVITATION
On the morning of a dance, girls watched hopefully for the young men who rode to each house, inviting the young people there to the dance.

A young man might serenade his sweetheart with guitar or violin music.

ENGAGEMENT

To become officially engaged, the couple knelt before the bride's godfather. He slipped a rosary first over the boy's head, then over the girl's.

Before the wedding, girls sprinkled mint leaves and flower petals on the ground. They released lovely scents when stepped on.

Rosary

RUNAWAY BRIDE

Parents usually chose a husband for their daughter. Most girls obeyed their parents and married the man chosen for them. A daring daughter might *elope*, or run away to marry the young man *she* loved!

CELEBRATION

After the wedding, the bride and groom and their godparents, family, and friends enjoyed a dance and grand feast that could last for days.

SQUASH!

To refuse an offer of marriage, a young girl's family sent the boy's family a squash!

Fashion

Most of the time, girls and women wore loose, practical work clothes. The colors and patterns they wore were inspired by the New Mexico landscape itself and created a look that was uniquely New Mexican. But for special occasions, girls and women loved to dress up in the fancy fashions of Europe and Mexico, with finery imported from around the world!

A shawl called a **rebozo** *(reh-BO-so) shaded a girl's face from the strong New Mexican sun.*

From the book Changes for Josefina

SARAPE
New Mexicans wore thick wool *sarapes* (sah-RAH-pehs), or ponchos, in winter. If the outside of the sarape got wet, the yarn swelled, stopping the water from soaking through.

DRESSED FOR THE DAY
A loose white blouse and calf-length skirt suited a girl's active lifestyle.

A small leather pouch was worn at the waist.

Petticoat hems were often finished with fancy edges or with lace.

MOCCASINS
Pueblo Indians wore comfortable, sturdy moccasins, a style settlers began to wear, too.

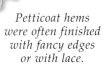

FRINGES
Girls and women sometimes created elaborate patterns and textures with the fringes of their sashes.

SEWING DIARY
A fashionable woman in Mexico City might have kept notes about the latest dress designs from Europe, just as Tía Dolores did.

FANCY FILIGREE
New Mexican jewelers twisted metal threads into delicate designs, or *filigrees*.

WELL WRAPPED
A woman might complete a special outfit with an embroidered silk shawl. This shawl shows scenes from Mexico City.

These fancy curls are held in place with sugar water.

DRESSED FOR DANCING
For a *fandango* (fahn-DAHN-go), or dance party, a girl changed into a fancier skirt, perhaps trimmed with delicate ribbons and made of fine cotton that swayed gracefully as she danced.

On fancy occasions girls tied their braids with ribbon.

THE FINISHING TOUCH
For a special occasion, women often wore several pieces of jewelry at once. Metalsmiths made exquisite creations of gold, silver, pearls, coral, and precious stones.

Keeping Clean and Beautiful

In Josefina's day, few people in Mexico or the United States bathed, brushed their teeth, or even changed their clothes daily. But the women of New Mexico, despite the lack of water and the ever-present dust, worked hard to keep their homes, their families, and themselves clean and beautiful.

BRINGING WATER
The first chore of each day was carrying a large pottery jar down to the stream to get water for cooking, drinking, and washing.

YUCCA SUDS
New Mexican settlers most often used yucca root for soap. They pounded the root with a rock, and then swished it in water to make a soapy lather.

SUNSCREEN
Women wore mud on their faces to protect them from the strong sun. They also made makeup from powders mixed with water or sour milk. They scented it with herbs and flowers.

LAUNDRY
Women carried baskets of bedding, clothing, and rugs to the stream for washing. They spread clean clothes on bushes to dry.

PESKY PESTS
Lice—small insects that live on people's bodies—were common pests. Girls and women gathered to pick lice from one another's hair, just as these Pueblo women may be doing. If clothes were infested, they were spread on anthills. The ants quickly ate up the lice!

HAIR CARE
Both Pueblo Indians and New Mexican settlers made hairbrushes by tying stiff grasses or straw together.

LAYING THE DUST
Girls sprinkled water on the earthen floors to help "lay the dust." They swept the floor with brooms that were larger versions of hairbrushes.

CHAMBER POTS
At night, settlers used ceramic pots for toilets. They were emptied and cleaned out each morning.

25

Medicine and Health

In a time when keeping clean was not easy, diseases spread quickly. In those days, people did not understand that germs or bacteria caused sickness and that diseases could be passed by sharing dirty dishes, clothes, and other items. When illness struck, each housewife had a store of home remedies to try. When those didn't work, villagers went to a *curandera* (koo-rahn-DEH-rah) like Tía Magdalena, who was skilled in making medicines.

HOT HEALING
Chiles contain a chemical that heats without burning the skin and stops pain without killing nerves. Medicines made from chiles eased pain, helped heal wounds, and cured frostbite.

SHEPHERD'S BED
A sick person or animal might sleep in the *shepherd's bed* above the kitchen hearth. It was the warmest spot in the house.

HERBAL CURES
Curanderas used mint leaves to ease stomachaches, ground pumpkin stems to soothe sore throats, and a plant called *inmortal* (een-mor-TAHL) to make a person sneeze and sneeze a cold away!

GIVING THANKS
In this painting, a father gives thanks to Saint Raymond, the patron saint of childbirth, for the safe delivery of his healthy baby.

EX. VOTO.

The Dreaded Pox

In the 1600s and 1700s, almost everyone caught smallpox sooner or later. The first sign was a high fever. Then a red rash covered the face, hands, and feet. The rash turned into pus-filled bumps called *pox*. Today, doctors know how to prevent this deadly disease. But in Josefina's time, people were just learning.

In 1801, the Spanish king learned about a new medical process called *inoculation* (in-ok-yuh-LAY-shun) that protected people from smallpox. A doctor passed a needle and thread through one of the pox and then through the skin of a healthy person. This gave the healthy person a mild case of smallpox that he or she could fight off. People who recovered from smallpox never caught it again.

The king sent an "expedition against smallpox" to travel around the world. Doctors traveled with young orphans who were infected with mild cases of smallpox. The fluid in their pox was transferred by needle and thread to people needing inoculation.

When the expedition reached New Mexico, local orphans were recruited to travel with the doctors. These children spread the first smallpox inoculations to the small villages of New Mexico, preventing hundreds of deaths.

From the book Happy Birthday, Josefina!

Josefina hoped to be a curandera one day, just like Tía Magdalena.

ASKING FOR HELP
If a girl hurt her leg, she might pin a medal in the shape of a leg to a saint's statue to ask for healing.

People prayed to Saint Raphael for good health.

Life of Danger

Disease was just one of many dangers that threatened the lives of New Mexicans. Droughts killed crops and animals, leaving settlers without enough food. But too much rain could turn small streams into raging rivers that flooded the fields and drowned the animals. Indian raids and wild animals also took their toll. Settlers prayed to God and the saints for safety and listened for the urgent clanging of the church bell, which meant danger, danger, danger!

DANGER!
A clanging church bell brought villagers running to help fight house fires, Indian attacks, or other threats. It also announced when someone had died.

INDIAN ATTACK
Settlers rode from rancho to rancho to warn of an Indian attack. Bands of Comanches, Apaches, and Navajos sometimes raided homes and farms, stole animals, and took people captive.

KEEPING WATCH
Rancho families kept watch for raiding Indians from their watchtowers.

CHILDHOOD DISEASES
Many children died from smallpox and other diseases. People wore white to children's funerals and carried colorful flags to show their belief that the child was safe in heaven.

Graves were usually marked by simple wooden crosses.

SAINT BARBARA

New Mexicans offered this prayer to Saint Barbara, protector against lightning and storms:

Saint Barbara, holy maid, save us, Lady, in thunder and lightning afraid!

DEATH FIGURE

The death figure reminded New Mexicans that death could come at any moment, so their hearts and souls should always be ready to meet God.

FLASH FLOODS

Flash floods could sweep away wagons and livestock. Caravans sometimes had to wait three months on the banks of the Rio Grande until it was safe for crossing.

BEARS

Bears raided ripe crops in the autumn, leaving the farmer's family without food for the winter. Bears sometimes killed farmers who were trying to protect their fields.

Poisonous rattlesnakes blended into the desert.

29

The Weeping Woman

With all the dangers of living in northern New Mexico, mothers kept a close watch on their children. At night in front of the fire, children gathered close to hear the spooky story of the Weeping Woman, La Llorona *(lah yo-RO-nah)*. It helped them remember to be inside before dark.

Many years ago, the story begins, a woman named María lived in town. She had everything she could want—riches, a handsome husband, and two beautiful children. One day the children were playing by the river and fell into the water. The boy and girl didn't know how to swim, and the current was strong. María tried desperately to save them, but she and her children drowned.

Soon after, the townspeople began to hear the sounds of crying at night. Some said it was just the wind. Others said it was María, crying for her children. From that night on, María was known as the Weeping Woman. Mothers warned their children to be home before dark because the Weeping Woman was looking for her children and might take them instead.

One boy disobeyed his mother and stayed out late one night. As he neared the riverbank, he heard a woman crying and calling for her children. Then a draped figure started walking toward him. She came closer and closer. The boy was so terrified he couldn't move. The Weeping Woman grabbed him and was taking him toward the  river when the church bell began to ring. Suddenly she dropped the boy and disappeared from sight. The boy ran home and told his family and all the villagers what he had seen.

Some say the Weeping Woman is make-believe, the storyteller would say. *But if you wander down to the river after dark, you might hear her crying, "Ay, ay, ay! Where oh where are my children?" So you must always be sure to come inside before dark!*

The Village

On the New Mexican frontier, settlers banded together in villages for protection against dangers. But they also came together in friendship, to practice their faith, and to provide food for their families. Villages were few and far between, so the settlers depended on their neighbors for all things. They worked together, worshiped together, celebrated and mourned together. The lives of the villagers were woven together tightly to form a close community.

ORCHARDS
Villagers tended nearby orchards of apricot, peach, apple, and pear trees, which early settlers brought from Spain.

WATERING CROPS
All the men in the village helped clean and repair the irrigation ditches, or *acequias* (ah-SEH-kee-ahs), that brought water to their crops.

Gates controlled the flow of water into the fields.

WORK
All the men in the village farmed, but some worked as carpenters, blacksmiths, and healers, too.

Metal was so rare that villagers donated copper pots and even gold and silver jewelry to be melted down and made into a church bell.

Most villagers were buried in the churchyard, but important people were sometimes buried right in the church.

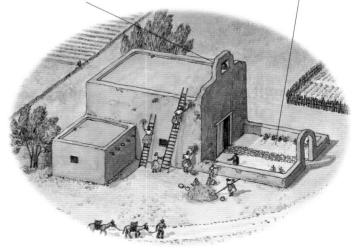

CHURCH
The church was the center of village life. Most churches faced east so that the rising sun provided light for morning Mass. Everyone in the village helped clean, decorate, and repair the church.

GARDENS
Villagers grew beans, squash, melons, chiles, and many other foods in their gardens. They preserved these foods so they could be eaten through the winter.

PLAZA
All the houses in the village faced a central square, or plaza. Villagers met there to do chores, visit, play, and trade.

Community Celebration

From the book *Josefina's Surprise*

LAS POSADAS

Las Posadas was Josefina's favorite community celebration. The whole village took part in acting out the story of Jesus' parents searching for lodging in Bethlehem on Christmas Eve.

Settlers worked hard to keep their families fed and protected on the New Mexican frontier. Celebrations were a welcome break from daily chores and a chance for villagers to come together in fun. New Mexicans celebrated many occasions, including weddings, Christmas and other religious holidays, and a successful harvest. One important celebration was the village saint's day. Each village had a patron saint and celebrated the saint's feast day. Like most celebrations, this one began with a church service in the morning and ended with a big meal and dancing through the night.

THE FARMER

Saint Isadore was the patron saint of many villages. Isadore was a farmer who had very deep faith. God rewarded him by sending an angel to do his plowing while he attended church. In spring, villagers carried statues of Saint Isadore to their fields as a way of asking God for a good harvest.

FOOD

The women worked together to prepare tortillas, spicy stews, meat pies, cookies, and other treats for big feasts.

THE SAINT'S DAY

The men of the village carried an image of the patron saint to the church, where the whole village asked for the saint's blessing. The village's church was usually named after the patron saint.

DECORATIONS

To prepare for a feast day, women and girls cleaned the church and decorated it with handmade flowers of cloth, paper, or even cornhusks.

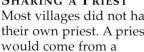

SHARING A PRIEST

Most villages did not have their own priest. A priest would come from a larger town, like Santa Fe, a few times a year or on special feast days to say Mass.

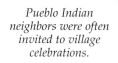

Pueblo Indian neighbors were often invited to village celebrations.

MUSIC

Celebrations usually ended with a dance, or *fandango*. Fiddlers, guitar players, and other musicians played Spanish and Mexican music for the guests, who often danced until dawn!

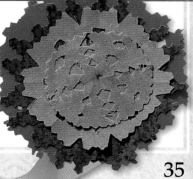

The Pueblo

By the time Josefina was a girl, the Pueblo Indians and Spanish settlers had been living as neighbors for many years. The Pueblo Indians were not a single group of people. They were several communities that shared a similar way of life—they all built adobe villages that the Spanish called *pueblos*, made beautiful pottery, and farmed. But each village had its own language, government, and customs.

FEATHERS AND FOOD
Pueblo Indians prized parrots from Mexico for their colorful feathers. They raised turkeys and chickens for food.

In good weather, people went about their daily activities outdoors on the pueblo's terraces.

TRAPDOORS
For protection, there were no outside doors on the ground floor. People entered these rooms through trapdoors in the ceiling.

SPOUTS
Spouts drained water off the flat roofs. Otherwise, it would collect there and cause leaks.

LADDERS
People used wooden ladders to climb to the upper stories. If an enemy attacked, they pulled up their ladders so no one could enter.

T DOORWAYS
Doorways in the upper stories were only four feet high. The T shape kept the opening small in case of attack, while still allowing a person carrying a bundle to pass through.

1 *In areas where there was a lot of traffic, people (and dogs!) used double ladders.*

2 *Men did much of the weaving, knitting, and embroidery.*

③ *Pueblo Indians were vegetarians most of the time—they had 40 different ways of cooking corn!*

WOMEN'S WORK
Women made the tools they needed to prepare food—grinding stones, ovens, pottery, baskets, and other goods. Women did most of the building, too, and the completed house belonged to them.

GRINDING CORN
Pueblo women ground corn into flour. They started with dried corn kernels on a rough stone and moved to smoother stones to grind the corn finer.

KIVAS
Pueblo men held religious ceremonies in underground rooms called *kivas* (KEE-vahs). They also used kivas as workrooms and places to meet and relax. Women were rarely allowed to enter kivas.

Taken Captive

The Spanish settlers and Pueblo Indians were friends and trading partners. Other Indians, such as the Comanche, Apache, and Navajo, raided Spanish settlements and Pueblo villages for horses and other goods. They also took women and children as captives.

The Spanish raided right back. They brought Indian captives to their homes and ranchos to live as servants. Some captives were treated with kindness, like one Navajo woman called Rosario (ro-ZAH-ree-oh).

For many years, Rosario was the servant of a priest named Padre Martínez (PAH-dreh mahr-TEE-nehs) in the town of Taos. He was very kind to her and even bought her baby daughter, who had been taken from Rosario when she

was captured. Still, Rosario tried several times over the years to escape to her people. But she was always found and taken back to Padre Martínez. Eventually, she stopped trying to run.

One day, Padre Martínez told Rosario she was free to go. At first, Rosario

was overjoyed at the thought of seeing her people again. Then sadly, she realized she no longer knew them. The only life she knew was with Padre Martínez. She thought about how much she would miss him and the life she had made for herself in Taos.

Rosario decided to stay with Padre Martínez. To thank him, she wove him a special sarape. She thought,

I'll make it a bit Navajo and the rest Spanish, for I am both now. I'll use more white for the pureness, nobleness and sincerity of the padre, and I'll use black for the sorrow I caused him and for the sorrow I too went through many years ago. And I'll put red for the courage we all have to have.

Home at Last

Refugio (reh-FOO-hee-oh) was a young Spanish woman who had lived as a captive among several Indian tribes since she was 15 years old. After several years, she was sold to the Apaches. There, she found another captive who spoke Spanish. Together, they escaped.

Refugio made it to a military fort, where the captain and his wife took her in. There, she fell in love with and married a soldier. The soldier sent for his brothers to take his new wife to his family's house in Taos, where she would live until he got out of the army.

The brothers were polite, but quiet. As they rode to Taos, Refugio grew nervous. How would her husband's family and friends receive her? Would they be mistrustful of her because she'd lived so long among Indians?

As they neared Taos, the church bell suddenly began to ring, and Refugio could see the townspeople gathering. What could this mean? She bravely rode into the plaza and got down from her horse. At first, no one moved or spoke. Then slowly, some people stepped forward and embraced her warmly. Others threw pieces of silver at her feet as a sign of welcome. Refugio had found a home at last.

El Camino Real

One of the most exciting events of the year was the arrival of a trading caravan. Each year Josefina's grandfather led a caravan of hundreds of cart drivers, traders, soldiers, and whole families of travelers from Santa Fe to Mexico City and back again. They followed the 1,600-mile wagon trail called the Camino Real. The trail crossed hot, dry deserts, steep mountains and canyons, and swift rivers. Traders made the dangerous ten-month trip once a year to bring mail, news, supplies, and treasures from around the world to the small communities of northern New Mexico.

① **Muleteers,** or men who handled the mules, were greatly trusted. People sent gold, silver, and other valuables with them on the trail.

② The wooden wheels of the carts squeaked so loudly they could be heard for miles.

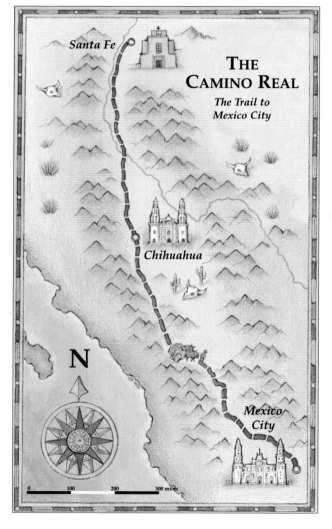

THE
CAMINO REAL
The Trail to
Mexico City

Santa Fe

Chihuahua

N

Mexico
City

0   100   200   300 miles

BACK AND FORTH
Traders brought goods such as blankets and animal hides from Santa Fe to Mexico City. There, they loaded up with supplies needed in New Mexico, such as iron tools, and luxuries like chocolate and European lace.

Leather trunks were lighter than wood and more flexible for packing.

SPUR THEM ON!
If horses or mules were moving too slowly, riders and drivers used spurs to make them move faster.

Dead Man's Journey

Travelers on the Camino Real had to cross a nearly waterless stretch of desert in southwestern New Mexico now known as "The Route of the Dead Man." One of the only sources of water is a spring called "The Pools of the Little Dog." The spring got that name when the first Spanish settlers crossed the desert in 1598. By their second day in the desert, the settlers were almost out of water. That evening, a dog returned to camp with mud on its paws and muzzle. A soldier followed the paw prints in the sand and found the spring, saving the settlers' lives.

③ *Soldiers helped protect caravans from attacks by Indians and bandits.*

ON THE TRAIL
Men who traveled often took their entire families with them rather than leave them at home unprotected.

IN THE SADDLE
Many saddles had intricate leather tooling and shiny silver trim. But no matter how beautiful the saddle, it wasn't comfortable to sit on for eight or ten hours a day!

Mexico City

In 1824, Mexico City was the capital of Mexico and the most important city in North America. Mexicans, Indians, Africans, and Spaniards and other Europeans lived and mingled in the city. By day, street vendors filled the main plaza. By night, citizens flocked to theaters, dances, and the city's many gambling houses. Mexico City was rich, crowded, dirty, sophisticated, and by far the most exciting place in all of Mexico!

Elegant young ladies rode in carriages around Alameda Park, the place to be seen in Mexico City.

Magnificent statues of plumed serpents guarded the Aztec empire.

THE AZTEC EMPIRE

Mexico City was built on the site of the capital city of the Aztec Indian empire. The city had glittering pyramids and a marketplace where 60,000 people bought and sold goods. It was destroyed during fighting with the Spanish in the 1500s.

Mexican coins from the 1800s

*People who couldn't write paid **scribes** to write their letters for them in the plaza.*

HEAVENLY DETAILS
Artistic details like this finely sculpted angel graced the many churches of Mexico City.

BEAUTIFUL BUILDINGS
Mexico City was known for its dazzling buildings. Some were as richly decorated as wedding cakes!

BEASTS OF BURDEN
The streets of Mexico City were often too crowded for wagons, so people were hired to carry bundles as heavy as 300 pounds. During the rainy season, they were hired to carry the wealthy across puddles!

HEART OF THE CITY
The main plaza was the heart of Mexico City. Each day, hundreds of vendors and shoppers filled the plaza. Mexicans could buy anything from scissors to children's books to vegetables at the market.

A World of Goods

Great sailing ships docked in the ports of southern Mexico. They carried treasures from every corner of the world—China, the Philippines, France, England, Spain, and South America. These goods traveled by wagon to Mexico City, then up the Camino Real to New Mexico. A settler in even the most remote village of New Mexico could own a bit of lace from Belgium or a silk shawl from China!

This embroidered silk shawl, called a **mantón** *(mahn-TOHN), came from China.*

HAIR COMBS
Tortoiseshell combs came from Spain and France. Their wide teeth secured them to the back of the head, while the fancy top stood above like a crown.

This graceful French fan unfolds to show a delicate arc of tortoiseshell and lace.

CORAL NECKLACE
Artists in Spain made coral necklaces with religious medals to be worn at weddings and other religious occasions.

BEADED PURSE
Girls and women tied purses around their waists. This purse from Spain is beaded with birds and flowers.

SILK SLIPPERS
Light, elegant silk slippers from Mexico were designed for dancing!

Mexican artists were inspired by styles from all over the world. The blue background on this plate is an Asian style, and the flowers are European.

CANDLESTICK

Candlesticks were first imported to New Mexico for churches. They were soon used in houses as well.

PARROT

Parrots from Central America sometimes traveled with traders to New Mexico. Pueblo Indians prized them for their brilliant feathers.

GOURD CUP

Silversmiths in Peru made cups that combined hollowed-out nuts and gourds with silver details.

Ships from Spain brought both pots and pottery makers to Mexico.

Women's Rights

At a time when an American woman's only place was in the home, New Mexican women enjoyed many more rights and freedoms. Though men were still in charge in 1824, women kept their maiden names after marriage, could own property and businesses, did not have to give their money to their husbands, and could pass down property to their daughters. American women wouldn't have those rights for years!

MAKING CHANGE
Women set up stalls in town plazas to sell items they had made and food they had grown. Women also worked outside the home as bakers, weavers, seamstresses, shepherds, and midwives.

TAKING CHARGE
Women could write wills and inherit property. Though one woman named Doña Refugio was no older than 14 when she married, she managed her husband's rancho so well that he wrote a will putting her in charge in the event of his death.

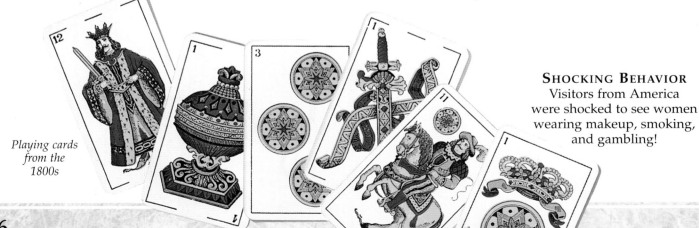

Playing cards from the 1800s

SHOCKING BEHAVIOR
Visitors from America were shocked to see women wearing makeup, smoking, and gambling!

A Woman of Independence

One of the wealthiest citizens of Santa Fe in the 1830s and 1840s was a woman—Doña Gertrudis Barceló. When La Tules (lah TOO-lehs), as she was known, was forced into an unhappy marriage at an early age, she ran away to Santa Fe. There she opened a gambling house. New Mexicans loved to play a card game called *monte* (MOHN-teh). In monte, a player bets on his or her luck against a dealer. The most skilled card dealer

Santa Fe

in Santa Fe was La Tules, who played the cards "as steadily as though she were handling only a knitting needle," as one American journalist recalled. During the war between the United States and Mexico in the 1840s, both Mexican and American soldiers came to her establishment to dance, gamble, and talk politics. La Tules was a trusted adviser to both.

La Tules became famous as the woman who dared to do men's work. But she also worked for the church, gave generously to the poor, and took in orphans to raise. La Tules was a New Mexican woman of true spirit and independence.

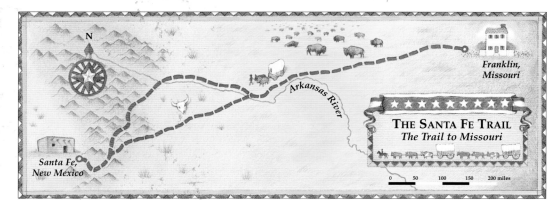

The Santa Fe Trail
The Trail to Missouri

Franklin, Missouri

Arkansas River

Santa Fe, New Mexico

N

0   50   100   150   200 miles

The Santa Fe Trail

In 1821, when Mexico won independence from Spain, it set up a new government and threw out the old Spanish laws—including the one forbidding trade with the United States. Within months, Americans began forging a road over the prairies and mountains from Missouri to Santa Fe. It became known as the Santa Fe Trail. Soon New Mexican trade caravans were making the trip, too, taking items from New Mexico into the United States. But the traders brought more than goods. They brought new ideas and ways of doing things. The trail became a link between two nations—Mexico and the United States—and both would be changed forever.

American trade wagons were brilliant red, white, and blue.

THE JOURNEY

The Santa Fe Trail crossed more than 800 miles of bone-dry deserts and high, treacherous mountains. From Santa Fe, American wagon trains often continued south along the Camino Real to trade in the larger Mexican cities.

HERE THEY COME!

Trade wagons swept across the desert to Santa Fe. People called the wagons *prairie schooners* because their white canvas roofs looked like the sails on ships called *schooners*.

PULL!

Slow but steady, a team of eight oxen could pull a wagon weighing more than two tons. Mules were stronger and ate less, but they could be ornery. One man joked that a mule could stand on one leg and kick with the other three!

ARRIVING IN SANTA FE

Traders stopped just outside of Santa Fe to comb their hair and change into clean shirts before pulling into the plaza. Many New Mexicans were excited to see the Americans, but others didn't trust the foreigners.

TRADE GOODS

New Mexicans were eager for the new items Americans brought, such as calico cloth, glass bottles, toys, mirrors, machine-made clothing, tools, and shoes. The American goods were also cheaper than those brought up the Camino Real.

Life on the Trail

By the time Josefina was a young woman in the 1840s, hundreds of wagons were traveling the Santa Fe Trail. In the early days, only men made the journey, but now some wagons were bringing women and children. The first American woman on the trail was Mary Donoho. She followed the Santa Fe Trail with her husband and baby daughter in 1833. These trips were full of danger—there were violent storms on the open plains, deep rivers to cross, waterless stretches, and occasional attacks by Indians. Despite this, many women loved the adventure of life on the trail.

We drove the wagons 18 hours a day. That left only 6 hours for sleep. We were always tired. Sometimes at noon we got a short nap. But the mules would begin braying and wake us up. We called the mules "alarm clocks."
— José Garule, 16 years old, 1867

JAM-PACKED!
Inside their wagons, families packed food, trade goods, and everything else they'd need for the two-month journey to New Mexico.

Susan Magoffin was an 18-year-old bride when she followed the trail in 1846.

American girls and women wore bonnets to shade their faces and prevent an unfashionable tan.

MIRAGE
Marion Russell recalled a desert *mirage*, or illusion from the heat: "Sometimes it would look like a party of attacking Indians, and the women would cry and begin counting their children."

Marion Russell

In 1852, 7-year-old Marion Russell and her mother and brothers set out from Kansas for the Southwest on a Santa Fe Trail wagon train. Throughout her life, Marion would travel along the Santa Fe Trail many times, but she never forgot that first trip. When she was a very old woman, she described the trip in her memoirs:

Mules draw a wagon a bit more gently than horses, but oxen are best of all. 'Tis true that they walk slowly, but there is a rhythm in their walking that sways the great wagons gently. Often, when I got tired of sitting on the hard spring seat by Mother, I would crawl back among the blankets, where I would play with my doll or fall asleep.

Each noon we would halt for a brief hour's rest. I can see the tired drivers at noonday lying under the shade of the wagons, their hats covering their faces as they slept. I can see the tired, sweaty mules rolling over and over in the grass, delighted to be free from the heavy wagons.

Each night there were two great circles of wagons. Between them was a bit of no-man's land which the children used as a playground. The ball games that went on there! The games of leapfrog and dare base. One night I lingered long alone in little no-man's land to gather a species of white poppy that bloomed only at night.

The camp was astir at daybreak. Sunbonnets bobbed merrily over cooking fires, on the air a smell of coffee. Packing was done swiftly and the mules hitched to the wagons. Then the children were counted and loaded. A swift glance about to see that nothing was left behind, and we were off for another day on the trail.

At the end of the day, my chore was to gather the buffalo chips to fuel the cooking fire. I would stand back and kick them, then reach down and gather them carefully, for under them lived big spiders and centipedes. I would fill my long, full dress skirt with the evening's fuel and take it back to Mother.

After we had traveled for what seemed like an eternity across the hot, dry land, we awoke one morning to find the air filled with a cool, misty rain. Someway it seemed we had entered a strange land of enchantment. Captain Aubry told us we were now in New Mexico Territory.

Then we passed through a great wooden gateway that arched high above us. We moved along narrow alley-like streets past iron-barred windows. We were among a scattering of low, square-cornered adobe houses. Our caravan wriggled through donkeys, goats and Mexican chickens. Dogs barked at us. Big-eyed children stared at us. Black-shawled women smiled shyly at us. We were in Santa Fe.

Excerpted from *Land of Enchantment: Memoirs of Marion Russell along the Santa Fe Trail*

Kit and Josefa

Many American traders married New Mexican women and settled in New Mexico. One of the most famous of these couples was Kit and Josefa Carson.

Kit Carson ran away from his Missouri home and joined a Santa Fe wagon train at age 16. He lived alone in the wilderness trapping animals, and worked as a guide and scout in the uncharted West, where he encountered enemy Indian tribes, raging storms, and wild animals. But the slight, fair-haired frontiersman was perhaps never as nervous as the day he asked Don Francisco Jaramillo of Taos for his daughter's hand in marriage. Señorita Josefa Jaramillo was a strikingly beautiful young lady of 14, with heavy braids and great dark eyes. Surely her parents would prefer that Josefa marry a young man from Taos, not an American mountain man twice her age. But in February 1843, Kit and Josefa were married.

AN ADVENTURER AT HEART
Josefa soon learned how unpredictable life could be with the country's greatest adventurer. Soon after the wedding, Kit was off on a yearlong expedition to California.

Kit received this pipe and beaded tobacco pouch from the Ute Indians.

A YOUNG BEAUTY
A writer described Josefa when she was 19: *"Her beauty was of the haughty, heartbreaking kind, such as would lead a man with the glance of an eye to risk his life for one smile."*

FABRIC OF LOVE
Kit returned to Josefa whenever he could. Their times together were all the more precious because they were so rare. Each time he went away, he brought back beautiful fabric for Josefa.

Dress belonging to Josefa

*Josefa kept a **miniature**, or keepsake picture, of Kit. In the first six years of their marriage, Kit and Josefa lived together less than six months.*

A DEVOTED MOTHER
At home in New Mexico, Josefa raised their seven children, as well as several adopted Indian children.

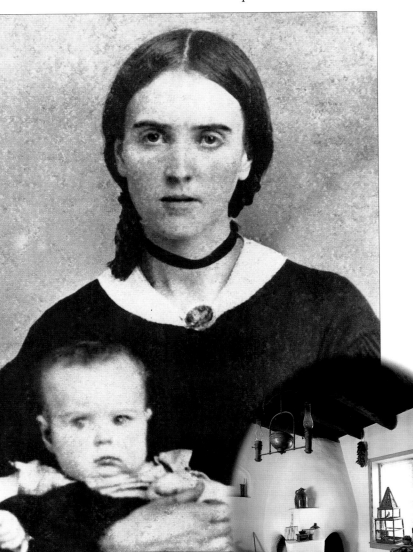

Josefa made meals for ten or more family members each day in this kitchen.

OFF TO WAR
In the 1860s, Kit went to fight in the Civil War. In his adventures and far-flung travels across half a continent, Kit risked his life to complete his missions and return home to Josefa, his "Little Jo."

Kit took this rifle with him when he went to fight in the Civil War.

END OF THE JOURNEY
Josefa died in April 1868, just days after the birth of their daughter Josefita. A month to the day after her death, Kit died. They had been married 25 years.

Santa Fe Market

Many cultures came together in Santa Fe, the biggest town in New Mexico. It was the seat of government for New Mexico, as well as a center of trade. Caravans traveling on the Camino Real as well as those on the Santa Fe Trail landed in the Santa Fe plaza. There New Mexicans, American traders, French mountain men, and Pueblo, Navajo, Apache, and other Indians traded goods. The Santa Fe plaza was always busy, but when trading caravans arrived it was an especially wild and colorful place, full of marvelous sights and interesting people.

PALACE OF THE GOVERNORS
The government building in Santa Fe, called the Palace of the Governors, was built of adobe around 1610.

SETTLERS
Settlers like Papá traded chiles, pine nuts, geese, chickens, blankets, and mules from their ranchos.

MOUNTAIN MAN
Mountain men, who were usually French or American, lived alone in the rugged mountains, trapping animals such as beavers. They brought the valuable animal pelts to the market to trade.

CUSTOMS HOUSE
Traders had to stop at the customs house to pay taxes on the goods they brought into New Mexico.

PRIEST
The priest was a highly respected member of any New Mexican community and often the only educated man in a small town.

PUEBLO INDIANS
Indians brought garden fruits and vegetables, pottery, blankets, and buffalo hides to trade.

LANDOWNER
This New Mexican landowner is dressed in a traditional outfit of a short jacket and pants that button up the side. Men left their pants unbuttoned part way up, showing their long white underpants underneath.

Becoming Americans

As trade between the United States and Mexico increased and more Americans began settling in New Mexico, the U.S. government began to feel that these lands should belong to the United States. In fact, many Americans believed that the United States should have all the land between the Atlantic and Pacific Oceans, an idea called *Manifest Destiny*. When Mexico refused to sell its northern lands, the United States declared war in 1845.

CELEBRATION
Others believed New Mexico would have a better future as part of America. They threw a fandango in honor of the new government.

TAKING SANTA FE
In August 1846, American soldiers marched into New Mexico and, without fighting any battles, claimed it for the United States. All New Mexicans—except Indians—became U.S. citizens.

WEEPING AND WAILING
Some New Mexicans feared their traditions would be lost forever under the new American government. When the American flag was raised over Santa Fe, women wailed so piercingly that even the cheering American soldiers fell silent.

HARVEY GIRLS
Single, adventurous young women went west to become "Harvey Girls." They served meals to tired and hungry travelers along the Santa Fe Railway.

Train tourists bought pottery from Pueblo Indians.

WAR
The Mexican War was fought south and west of New Mexico until 1848. When the war ended, the United States had taken half a million square miles of land that had belonged to Mexico.

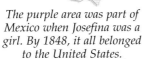

The purple area was part of Mexico when Josefina was a girl. By 1848, it all belonged to the United States.

RAILROAD
On February 9, 1880, the first train steamed into Santa Fe, following the old Santa Fe Trail in many places. The trail now brought thousands of tourists, who came to see the art and cultures of New Mexico.

A NEW LOOK
By the 1890s, most New Mexican women—like the writer Cleofas Jaramillo, shown here—had adopted American fashions.

A Peek into the Future

"*So many americano traders are coming to New Mexico now, with their different manners and customs and language!*" *Abuelita shook her head.* "*I fear our most precious beliefs will be lost if we don't do all we can to teach them to our children.*"

—Changes for Josefina

❊

Josefina, like many New Mexicans, lived under three different governments—first Spanish, then Mexican, and finally, when she was 33 years old, American. Change swept through New Mexico in her lifetime. In 1815, Josefina was born into a world that had changed little for more than 200 years. But in 1821, when Mexico won independence from Spain and opened its borders to foreigners, the American way of life began to seep into New Mexico. What would this have meant for Josefina?

By the time Josefina was ten years old, she was already using goods imported from the United States. She had met one American, a young trader, and likely would meet more. She or one of her sisters might even marry an American.

By the time Josefina was raising her own children, she might have had glass windows, wallpaper, and some American-style furniture. By the time she was a grandmother, she had probably traded her comfortable, loose-fitting blouses and skirts for the tight corsets and full hoopskirts of American fashions.

But if Josefina could come back to New Mexico today, she would be happy to find that although much has changed, many of the New Mexican traditions and customs of her childhood live on. Josefina could still walk among houses made of adobe, hear Spanish being spoken, smell chiles roasting over a fire, and see people celebrating their town's saint's day. New Mexico, like Josefina and her family, welcomed change while holding on to what was precious from the past.